New Creations
ADULT COLORING
BOOK SERIES

To see original photographs
please go to:

www.facebook.com/groups/newcreationscoloring

*"...the old is gone, all things
are are made new."*

2 Cor. 5:17

New Creations
ADULT COLORING
BOOK SERIES

This Book
Belongs To:

_____

_____

Date

*"...the old is gone, all things
are are made new."*

2 Cor. 5:17

Other coloring books are available from

New Creations Coloring Book Series:

- A DAY AT BUSCH GARDENS
- ABANDONED
- ANIMALS
- A COLORING MIX
- A DAY AT THE ZOO
- ARCHITECTURE
- ART DECO
- AVIARY GARDENS
- BABES AND TOTS
- BEACHES & SHORELINES
- BEAUTIFUL BRIDGES
- BEST OF NEW CREATIONS
- BIBLE STORIES VOLUME 1
- BIRDS
- CAROUSELS
- CHRISTMAS
- CHRISTMAS CARDS
- COUPLES
- DINOSAURS
- EASTER
- FALL
- FASHION
- FASHION: EDWARDIAN ERA
- FASHION: VICTORIAN BALLROOM
- FLOWERS
- FLOWERS II
- FLOWERS MINI
- FRACTALIUS ART
- FRACTALS
- FUN CHARACTERS
- FUSION
- GEMSTONES
- GRANDPARENTS
- GREETING CARDS
- HEARTS
- HOLIDAY

- HYMNS
- INSECTS
- KIDS
- MOMS
- NATURE
- OLD CHURCHES
- OIL PAINTINGS
- PAINTED CHRISTMAS CARDS
- PEOPLE
- REFLECTIONS
- ROARING 20'S
- SANTA
- SCENIC
- SCRIPTURES
- SEALIFE
- SEASONS
- SNOWMEN
- SPRING
- STREET ART
- STRUCTURAL ODDITIES
- THANKSGIVING
- THE ART OF AUTUMN
- TRANSPORTATION
- TROPICAL
- VICTORIAN CHRISTMAS
- VINTAGE CHRISTMAS
- VINTAGE CHRISTMAS CARDS
- VINTAGE BRIDES
- VINTAGE POST CARDS
- VINTAGE POST CARDS MINI
- VINTAGE PRINTS: CHILDREN
- VINTAGE STILL LIFE
- WATER
- WEEKLY CALENDAR
- WEEKLY PLANNER MINI
- WINTER

Be sure to collect them all.

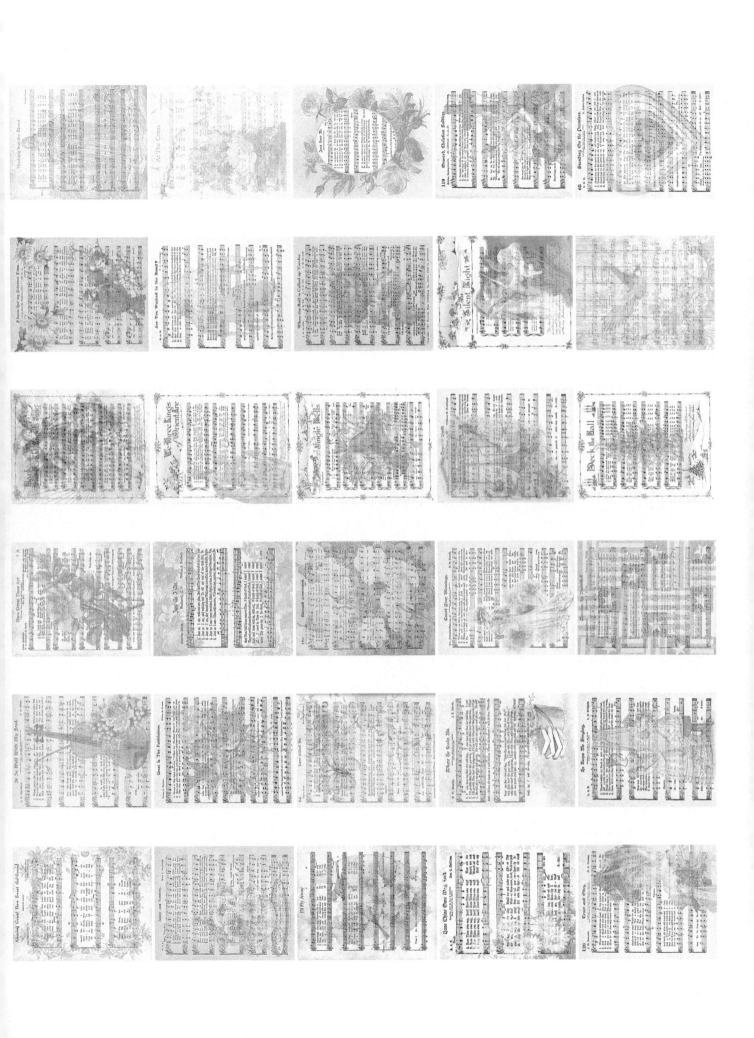

Dr. Teresa Davis has her doctorate degree in counseling and is the Executive Director of a non-profit Christian counseling center. As a counselor, she learned how coloring helps reduce stress, increase focus, minimize pain, and encourages imagination. As a lifetime amateur photographer she has a library of photos including over 100,000 pictures she has taken since receiving her first DSLR camera as a gift in 2007. In 2016, Teresa was intrigued when she saw her first grayscale coloring page, realizing she had a pot of grayscale gold contained within several external hard drives. New Creations Adult Coloring Book Series is the result of many hours searching through those hard drives to find just the right shots from photos she has taken during her worldwide travels.

Teresa has been married to her husband Brad for 40 years. They have 2 married sons and 4 teenage grandsons. She is also crafter of all sorts, seamstress, quilter, and recycler. In addition, she is a licensed and ordained minister, a public speaker, conference and retreat leader, and teacher.

Amazing Grace! How Sweet the Sound

AMAZING GRACE

JOHN NEWTON, 1725-1807

Early American Melody
Virginia Harmony, 1831

It Is Well With My Soul.

H. G. Spafford.

P. P. Bliss.

How Great Thou Art

"O Lord, how great are thy works!"
—Psa. 92:5

CARL BOBERG
Tr. by STUART K. HINE

O STORE GUD. *Irregular with Refrain*
Swedish Folk Melody
Arr. by STUART K. HINE

1. O, Lord, my God! When I in awe-some won-der Con-sid-er
2. When thru the woods and for-est glades I wan-der And hear the
3. And when I think, that God, His Son not spar-ing, Sent Him to
4. When Christ shall come with shout of ac-cla-ma-tion And take me

all the worlds Thy hands have made; I see the stars, I hear the roll-ing
birds sing sweet-ly in the trees; When I look down from lof-ty moun-tain
die, I scarce can take it in; That on the cross, my bur-den glad-ly
home, what joy shall fill my heart! Then I shall bow in hum-ble ad-o-

thun-der, Thy pow'r thru-out the u-ni-verse dis-played,
gran-deur And hear the brook and feel the gen-tle breeze;
bear-ing, He bled and died to take a-way my sin;
ra-tion And there pro-claim, my God, how great Thou art!

CHORUS

Then sings my

soul, my Sav-ior God to Thee; How great Thou art, how great Thou art! Then sings my

soul, my Sav-ior God to Thee; How great Thou art! how great Thou art!

Hark The Herald Angels Sing

MAESTOSO

1. Hark! the her - ald an - gels sing, "Glo - ry to the new-born King;
2. Hail the heav'n-born Prince of Peace! Hail the Sun of right-eous-ness!

Peace on earth, and mer-cy mild; God and sin - ners rec-on-ciled."
Light and life to all He brings, Risen with heal-ing in His Wings.

Joy-ful, all ye na-tions rise, Join the tri-umph of the skies;
Mild He lays His glo-ry by, Born that man no more may die,

With an - gel - ic hosts pro-claim, "Christ is born in Beth-le-hem!"
Born to raise the sons of earth, Born to give them sec-ond birth.

Hark! the her - ald an - gels sing, "Glo - ry to the new-born King."

Felix Mendelssohn-Bartholdy is credited with the composition of this tuneful carol. The words are from the pen of Charles Wesley, brother of the fam-ous theologian, John Wesley.

2

Nothing but the Blood

Robert Lowry

Choir

1. What can wash a - way my sin? Noth - ing but the blood of Je - sus.
2. For my par - don this I see: noth - ing but the blood of Je - sus.
3. Noth - ing can for sin a - tone: noth - ing but the blood of Je - sus.
4. This is all my hope and peace: noth - ing but the blood of Je - sus.

What can make me whole a - gain? Noth - ing but the blood of Je - sus.
For my clean-sing this my plea: noth - ing but the blood of Je - sus.
Naught of good that I have done: noth - ing but the blood of Je - sus.
This is all my right - eous-ness: noth - ing but the blood of Je - sus.

Refrain

O pre - cious is the flow that makes me white as snow;

no o - ther fount I know; noth-ing but the blood of Je - sus.

Great Is Thy Faithfulness

Thomas O. Chisholm

William M. Runyan

1. "Great is Thy faith-ful-ness," O God my Fa-ther, There is no shad-ow of
2. Sum-mer and win-ter, and springtime and harvest, Sun, moon and stars in their
3. Par-don for sin and a peace that en-dur-eth, Thy own dear pres-ence to

turn-ing with Thee; Thou chang-est not, Thy com-pas-sions, they fail not;
cours-es a-bove, Join with all na-ture in man-i-fold wit-ness
cheer and to guide; Strength for to-day and bright hope for to-mor-row,

CHORUS

As Thou hast been Thou for-ev-er wilt be.
To Thy great faith-ful-ness, mer-cy and love. "Great is Thy faith-ful-ness!
Bless-ings all mine, with ten thou-sand be-side!

Great is Thy faithfulness!" Morning by morning new mer-cies I see; All I have

rall. - - -

need-ed Thy hand hath pro-vid-ed— "Great is Thy faithfulness," Lord, un-to me!

Just As I Am.

Charlotte Elliott.   *Woodworth. L. M.*   William B. Bradbury.

1. Just as I am, with-out one plea, But that Thy blood was shed for me, And
2. Just as I am, and wait-ing not To rid my soul of one dark blot, To
3. Just as I am, tho' tossed about With many a conflict, many a doubt, Fight-
4. Just as I am—poor, wretched, blind; Sight, riches, healing of the mind, Yea,
5. Just as I am—Thou wilt receive, Wilt welcome, pardon, cleanse, relieve; Be-

that Thou bidd'st me come to Thee, O Lamb of God, I come! I come!
Thee whose blood can cleanse each spot, O Lamb of God, I come! I come!
ings and fears with-in, with-out, O Lamb of God, I come! I come!
all I need in Thee to find, O Lamb of God, I come! I come!
cause Thy prom-ise I be-lieve, O Lamb of God, I come! I come! A-MEN.

We Three Kings of Orient Are

SLOWLY

1. We three Kings of O - ri - ent are; Bear - ing gifts we trav - erse a - far
2. Born a King on Beth-le-hem's plain, Gold I bring to crown Him a - gain,
3. Frank-in-cense to of - fer have I; In - cense owns a De - i - ty nigh;
4. Myrrh is mine: its bit - ter per-fume Breathes a life of gath-er-ing gloom:
5. Glo-rious now be - hold Him a - rise, King and God and Sac - ri - fice;

Field and foun-tain, moor and mountain, Fol - low-ing yon - der star.
King for ev - er, ceas-ing nev - er O - ver us all to reign.
Prayer and prais-ing, all men rais-ing, Worship Him, God on high.
Sor-row-ing, sigh-ing, bleed-ing, dy - ing, Sealed in the stone-cold tomb.
Al - le - lu - ia, Al - le - lu - ia! Sounds thro' the earth and skies.

REFRAIN.

O Star of won - der, star of night, Star with roy - al beau - ty bright,

Westward lead-ing, still pro-ceed-ing, Guide us to Thy per-fect light.

This might well be called the first all-American carol, for both the words and music were written by an American clergyman, John Henry Hopkins, in 1857.

Are You Washed in the Blood?

E. A. H. E. A. HOFFMAN.

1. Have you been to Je - sus for the cleansing pow'r? Are you washed in the
2. Are you walk-ing dai - ly by the Sav-ior's side? Are you washed in the
3. When the Bridegroom cometh, will your robes be white, Pure and white in the
4. Lay a - side the garments that are stained with sin, And be washed in the

blood of the Lamb? Are you ful - ly trusting in His grace this hour? Are you
blood of the Lamb? Do you rest each moment in the Cru - ci-fied? Are you
blood of the Lamb? Will your soul be ready for the mansions bright And be
blood of the Lamb; There's a fountain flow-ing for the soul unclean, Oh, be

D. S.—*Are they white as snow? Are you*

FINE. CHORUS.

washed in the blood of the Lamb? Are you washed in the blood,

Are you washed in the blood,

washed in the blood of the Lamb?

D. S.

In the soul-cleansing blood of the Lamb? Are your garments spotless?

of the Lamb?

At The Cross

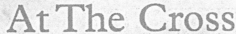

Isaac Watts
and Ralph E. Hudson

Ralph E. Hudson

A - las! and did my Sav - ior bleed? And
Was it for crimes that I have done He
Well might the sun in dark - ness hide And
But drops of grief can ne'er re - pay The

did my Sov - reign die? Would He de - vote that
groaned up - on the tree? A - maz - ing pit - y!
shut His glo - ries in. When Christ, the might - y
debt of love I owe. Here, Lord, I give my -

sa - cred head, For sin - ners such as I? At the
grace un - known! And love be - yond de - gree!
Mak - er died For man, the crea - ture's sin.
self a - way, 'Tis all that I can do!

cross, and the cross where I first saw the light And the

bur - den of my heart rolled a - way, It was there by faith I re -

ceived my sight, and now I am hap - py all the day!

I'll Fly Away

64 Love Lifted Me

JAMES ROWE   HOWARD E. SMITH

1. I was sink-ing deep in sin, Far from the peaceful shore, Ver-y deep-ly
2. All my heart to Him I give, Ev-er to Him I'll cling, In His bless-ed
3. Souls in dan-ger, look a-bove, Je-sus com-plete-ly saves; He will lift you

stained with-in, Sink-ing to rise no more; But the Mas-ter of the sea
pres-ence live, Ev-er His prais-es sing. Love so might-y and so true
by His love Out of the an—gry waves. He's the Mas-ter of the sea,

Heard my despairing cry, From the wa-ters lift-ed me, Now safe am I.
Mer-its my soul's best songs; Faith-ful, lov-ing serv-ice, too, To Him be-longs.
Bil-lows His will o-bey; He your Sav-ior wants to be—Be saved to-day.

CHORUS

Love lift-ed me! . . . . Love lift-ed me! . . . . When noth-ing
        e - ven me!   e - ven me!

else could help, Love lift-ed me. Love lift-ed me.

128 Blessed Assurance.

FANNY J. CROSBY.

MRS. JOS. F. KNAPP. By per.

1. Blessed as-sur-ance, Je-sus is mine! Oh, what a fore-taste of
2. Per-fect sub-mis-sion, per-fect de-light, Vis-ions of rap-ture now
3. Per-fect sub-mis-sion, all is at rest, I in my Sav-iour am

glo-ry divine! Heir of sal-va-tion, purchased of God, Born of His
burst on my sight; An-gels descending, bring from a-bove Ech-oes of
hap-py and blest; Watching and waiting, look-ing a-bove, Fill'd with His

CHORUS.

Spir-it, wash'd in His blood. This is my sto-ry, this is my
mer-cy, whispers of love.
goodness, lost in His love.

song, Prais-ing my Sav-iour all the day long; This is my sto-ry,

this is my song, Praising my Sav-iour all the day long.

113

Jingle Bells

ALLEGRO

J. PIERPONT

1. — Dash-ing thro' the snow In a one horse o-pen sleigh, —
2. A day or two a-go I thought I'd take a ride, And

o'er the fields we go, — Laugh-ing all the way;— The
soon Miss Fan-nie Bright Was seat-ed by my side;

Bells on bob-tail ring, — Mak-ing spir-its bright, What
horse was lean and lank, Mis-for-tune seem'd his lot, He

fun it is to ride and sing A sleigh-ing song to-night!
got in-to a drift-ed bank, And we, we got up-sot.

CHORUS

Jin-gle bells! jin-gle bells! Jin-gle all the way! Oh, what fun it is to ride in a

1. one-horse o-pen sleigh!

2. one-horse o-pen sleigh!

When the Roll is Called up Yonder.

J. M. BLACK   S. B. 958   B. T. B. 509   J. M. BLACK

1. When the trum-pet of the Lord shall sound, and time shall be no more,
2. On that bright and cloudless morn-ing when the dead in Christ shall rise,
3. Let us la - bor for the Mas - ter from the dawn till set of sun,

And the morning breaks, e - ter-nal bright and fair; When the saved of earth shall
And the glo - ry of His res - ur-rec-tion share: When His chos - en ones shall
Let us talk of all His wondrous love and care; Then when all of life is

gath - er o - ver on the oth - er shore, And the roll is called up yon - der,
gath - er to their home beyond the skies, And the roll is called up yon - der,
o - ver and our work on earth is done, And the roll is called up yon - der,

D. S.—roll is called up yon - der,

FINE. CHORUS.

I'll be there. When the roll is called up yon - der, When the roll is
When the roll is called up yon-der, I'll be there, When the roll is

I'll be there.

D. S.

called up yon - der, When the roll is called up yon - der, When the
called up yonder, I'll be there, When the roll is called up yon - der, When the

Have Thine Own Way, Lord.

A. A. P.
Slowly.

Geo. C. Stebbins.

1. Have Thine own way, Lord! Have Thine own way! Thou art the
2. Have Thine own way, Lord! Have Thine own way! Search me and
3. Have Thine own way, Lord! Have Thine own way! Wound-ed and
4. Have Thine own way, Lord! Have Thine own way! Hold o'er my

Pot-ter; I am the clay. Mould me and make me Aft-er Thy
try me, Mas-ter, to-day! Whit-er than snow, Lord, Wash me just
wear-y, Help me, I pray! Pow-er—all pow-er—Sure-ly is
be-ing Ab-so-lute-sway! Fill with Thy Spir-it Till all shall

will, While I am wait-ing, Yield-ed and still.
now, As in Thy pres-ence Hum-bly I bow.
Thine! Touch me and heal me, Sav-ior di-vine!
see Christ on-ly, al-ways, Liv-ing in me! A-MEN.

Where He Leads Me.

E. W. Blandly.

J. S. Norris.

1. I can hear my Sav-ior call-ing, I can hear my Sav-ior call-ing, I can
2. I'll go with Him thro' the gar-den, I'll go with Him thro' the gar-den, I'll go
3. I'll go with Him thro' the judgment, I'll go with Him thro' the judgment, I'll go
4. He will give me grace and glo-ry, He will give me grace and glo-ry, He will

REF.—Where He leads me I will fol-low, Where He leads me I will fol-low, Where He

hear my Sav - ior call-ing, "Take thy cross and fol-low, fol-low Me."
with Him thro' the gar-den, I'll go with Him, with Him all the way.
with Him thro' the judg-ment, I'll go with Him, with Him all the way.
give me grace and glo - ry, And go with me, with me all the way. A-MEN.

leads me I will fol-low, I'll go with Him. with Him all the way.

Count Your Blessings.

Rev. Johnson Oatman, Jr.

E. O. Excell.

1. When up-on life's bil-lows you are tem - pest-tossed, When you are dis-
2. Are you ev - er bur-dened with a load of care? Does the cross seem
3. When you look at oth-ers with their lands and gold, Think that Christ has
4. So, a - mid the con-flict, whether great or small, Do not be dis-

cour-aged, thinking all is lost, Count your man-y bless-ings, name them
heav - y you are called to bear? Count your man-y bless-ings, ev - 'ry
prom-ised you his wealth un - told; Count your man-y bless-ings, mon-ey
cour-aged, God is over all; Count your man-y bless-ings, an - gels

one by one, And it will sur-prise you what the Lord hath done.
count with doubt, And you will be sing-ing as the days go by.
can-not buy Your re-ward in Heav-en, nor your home on high.
will at-tend, Help and com-fort give you to your jour-ney's end.

Chorus.

Count your bless-ings, Name them one by one; Count your
Count your man-y bless-ings, Name them one by one; Count your man-y

bless-ings, Name them one by one; Count your bless-ings,
bless-ings, See what God hath done; Count your man-y bless-ings,

My Hope is Built.

Edward Mote. *The Solid Rock. L. M.* **William B. Bradbury.**

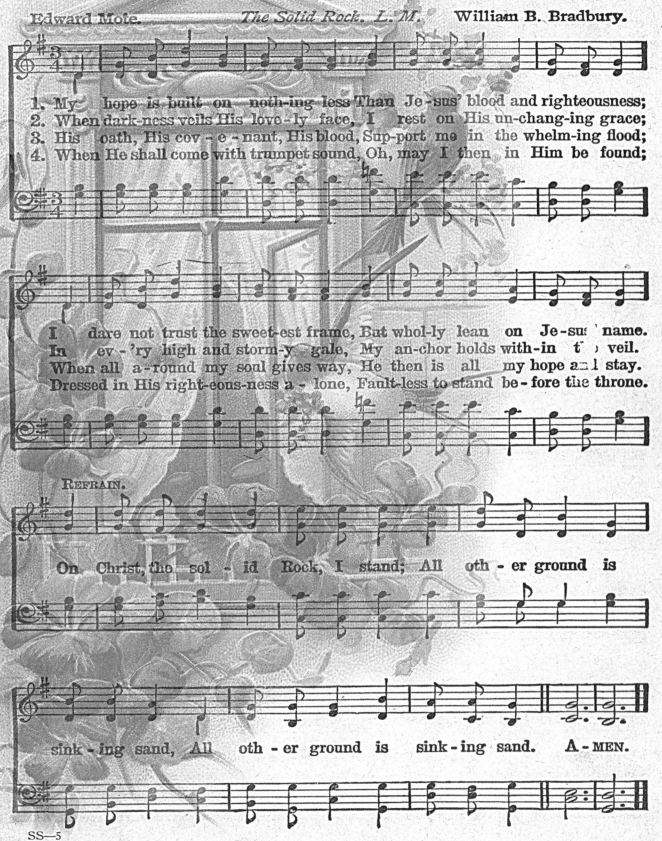

1. My hope is built on noth-ing less Than Je-sus' blood and righteousness;
2. When dark-ness veils His love-ly face, I rest on His un-chang-ing grace;
3. His oath, His cov-e-nant, His blood, Sup-port me in the whelm-ing flood;
4. When He shall come with trumpet sound, Oh, may I then in Him be found;

I dare not trust the sweet-est frame, But whol-ly lean on Je-sus' name.
In ev-'ry high and storm-y gale, My an-chor holds with-in the veil.
When all a-round my soul gives way, He then is all my hope and stay.
Dressed in His right-eous-ness a-lone, Fault-less to stand be-fore the throne.

REFRAIN.

On Christ, the sol-id Rock, I stand; All oth-er ground is

sink-ing sand, All oth-er ground is sink-ing sand. A-MEN.

Silent Night

SLOWLY, WITH EXPRESSION

Si - lent night, ho - ly night, All is calm, all is bright;
Si - lent night, ho - ly night, Dark-ness flees, all is light;
Si - lent night, ho - ly night, Won-drous Star, lend thy light;

Round yon Vir - gin Moth - er and Child, Ho - ly In-fant, so ten-der and mild,
Shep-herds near the an - gels sing, "Al-le-lu - ia! hail the King!
With the an - gels let us sing, Al - le-lu - ia to our King;

Sleep in heav - en - ly peace, Sleep in heav - en - ly peace.
Christ the Sav - ior is born! Christ the Sav - ior is born."
Christ the Sav - ior is born. Christ the Sav - ior is born.

Few literary products have known such a curious history as this best known and most beloved of all Christmas songs. Truly "inspired," it represents the combined efforts of Franz Gruber and Josef Mohr, schoolmaster and assistant priest, respectively, of the tiny Bavarian village of Oberndorf.

119 Onward, Christian Soldiers.

Sabine Baring-Gould. *St. Gertrude. 6s. 5s. D.* Arthur Sullivan.

1. Onward, Christian soldiers, Marching as to war, With the cross of Je - sus
2. At the sign of tri-umph Satan's host doth flee; On, then, Christian soldiers,
3. Like a might-y ar - my Moves the Church of God; Brothers, we are treading
4. Onward, then, ye people, Join our happy throng, Blend with ours your voices

Go - ing on be-fore! Christ, the roy-al Mas - ter, Leads a-gainst the foe;
On to vic-to - ry! Hell's foun-da-tions quiv-er At the shout of praise;
Where the saints have trod; We are not di - vid - ed; All one bod - y we,
In the tri-umph song; Glo-ry, laud, and hon - or, Un-to Christ the King;

REFRAIN.

For-ward in-to bat - tle, See, His banner go!
Brothers, lift your voices, Loud your anthems raise! Onward, Christian soldiers,
One in hope and doc-trine, One in char-i - ty.
This thro' countless a - ges Men and angels sing.

March-ing as to war, With the cross of Je-sus Go-ing on be-fore! A-MEN.

120 Trust and Obey.

J. H. Sammis.

D. B. Towner.

1. When we walk with the Lord In the Light of His Word What a glo-ry He
2. Not a shad-ow can rise, Not a cloud in the skies, But His smile quickly
3. Not a bur-den we bear, Not a sor-row we share, But our toil He doth
4. But we nev-er can prove The de-lights of His love Un-til all on the
5. Then in fel-low-ship sweet We will sit at His feet Or we'll walk by His

sheds on our way! While we do His good-will, He a-bides with us still,
drives it a-way; Not a doubt or a fear, Not a sigh nor a tear,
rich-ly re-pay; Not a grief nor a loss, Not a frown or a cross,
al-tar we lay; For the fa-vor He shows, And the joy He be-stows,
side in the way; What He says we will do, Where He sends we will go,—

CHORUS.

And with all who will trust and o-bey.
Can a-bide while we trust and o-bey.
But is blest if we trust and o-bey. Trust and o-bey, for there's no oth-er
Are for them who will trust and o-bey.
Nev-er fear, on-ly trust and o-bey.

way To be hap-py in Je-sus, But to trust and o-bey. A-men.

He Keeps Me Singing.

L. B. B.

L. B. Bridgers.

1. There's within my heart a mel-o-dy, Je-sus whis-pers sweet and low,
2. All my life was wrecked by sin and strife, Dis-cord filled my heart with pain,
3. Feast-ing on the rich-es of His grace, Rest-ing 'neath His shelt'ring wing,
4. Tho' sometimes He leads thro' waters deep, Tri-als fall a-cross the way,
5. Soon He's com-ing back to wel-come me Far be-yond the star-ry sky;

Fear not, I am with thee, peace, be still, In all of life's ebb and flow.
Je-sus swept across the broken strings, Stirred the slum-b'ring chords again.
Al-ways look-ing on His smil-ing face, That is why I shout and sing.
Tho' sometimes the path seems rough and steep, See His foot-prints all the way.
I shall wing my flight to worlds un-known, I shall reign with Him on high.

CHORUS.

Je-sus, Je-sus, Je-sus,— Sweet-est name I know,

Fills my ev-'ry long-ing, Keeps me sing-ing as I go. A-MEN.

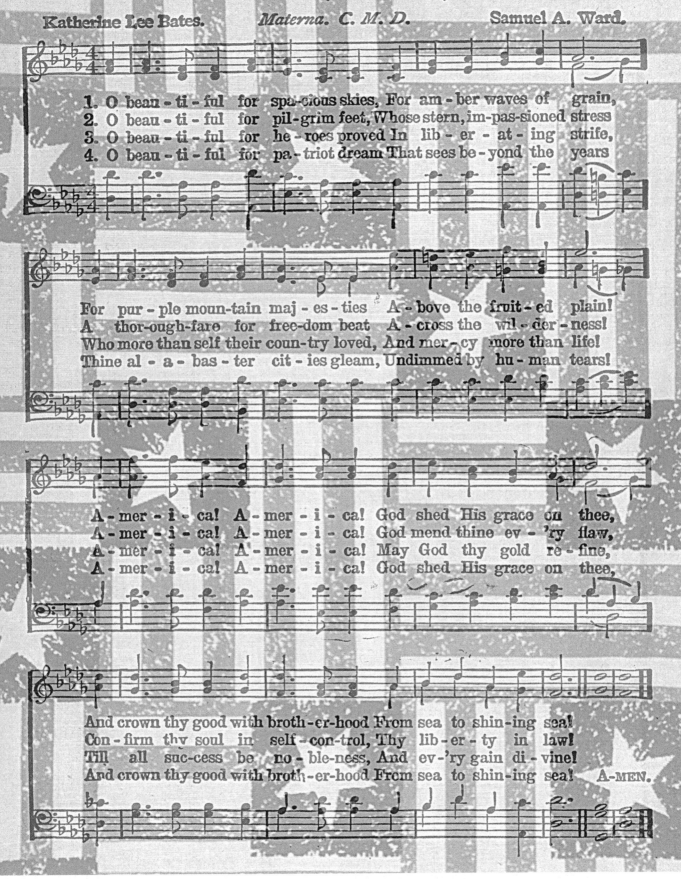

His Eye Is on the Sparrow

What a Friend we have in Jesus.

Rev. H. Bonar, D. D.

Karl Reden. By per.

1. What a friend we have in Je - sus, All our sins and griefs to bear;
2. Have we tri - als and temp - ta - tions? Is there trou - ble an - y - where?
3. Are we weak and heav - y la - den, Cumbered with a load of care?

What a priv - i - lege to car - ry Ev - 'ry-thing to God in prayer.
We should nev - er be dis - couraged, Take it to the Lord in prayer.
Pre - cious Sav - iour, still our ref - uge,— Take it to the Lord in prayer.

Oh, what peace we of - ten for - feit, Oh, what need-less pain we bear—
Can we find a friend so faith-ful, Who will all our sor-rows share?
Do our friends despise, for - sake us? Take it to the Lord in prayer;

All because we do not car - ry Ev - 'ry-thing to God in prayer.
Je - sus knows our ev - 'ry weakness, Take it to the Lord in prayer.
In His arms He'll take and shield us, We shall find a sol - ace there.

Just A Closer Walk With Thee

Traditional

Choir

I am weak but Thou art strong; Je - sus, keep me from all wrong;
Thro' this world of toil and snares, If I fal - ter, Lord, who cares?
When my fee - ble life is o'er, Time for me will be no more;

I'll be sa - tis-fied as long___ As I walk, let me walk close to Thee.
Who with me my bur-den shares?___ None but Thee, dear Lord, none but Thee.
Guide me gent-ly, safe - ly o'er___ To Thy king - dom shore, to Thy shore.

Just a clo-ser walk with Thee, Grant it, Je - sus, is my plea,___

Dai - ly wal-king close to Thee,___ Let it be, dear Lord, let it be.

O Little Town of Bethlehem

NOT TOO FAST

O lit-tle town of Beth-le-hem, How still we see thee lie!
For Christ is born of Ma - ry, And gath-ered all a - bove,
O ho - ly Child of Beth-le-hem! De-scend to us, we pray;

A - bove thy deep and dream-less sleep The si - lent stars go by;
While mor-tals sleep, the an - gels keep Their watch of won-dering love.
Cast out our sin, and en - ter in, Be born in us to day!

Yet in thy dark street shin - eth The ev - er - last - ing Light;
O morn-ing stars, to - geth - er Pro - claim the ho - ly birth,
We hear the Christ-mas an - gels The great glad tid - ings tell;

The hopes and fears of all the years Are met in thee to - night.
And prais-es sing to God our King, And peace to men on earth!
O come to us, a - bide with us, Our Lord Im-man - u - el!

Had not this extremely popular carol met with an instantaneous suc-
cess, its origin might have been lost to posterity because the author,
Phillips Brooks, in 1868, neglected to sign it.

The Old Rugged Cross *

G. B.

Geo. Bennard

1. On a hill far a-way stood an old rug-ged cross, The em-blem of
2. Oh, that old rug-ged cross so de-spised by the world, Has a wondrous at-
3. In the old rug-ged cross, stained with blood so di-vine, A won - drous
4. To the old rug-ged cross I will ev-er be true, Its shame and re-

suf-f'ring and shame; And I love that old cross where the dear-est and best
trac-tion for me; For the dear Lamb of God left His glo-ry a-bove,
beau-ty I see; For 'twas on that old cross Je-sus suf-fered and died,
proach gladly bear; Then He'll call me some day to my home far a-way,

CHORUS

For a world of lost sin-ners was slain.
To bear it to dark Cal - va - ry.
To par-don and sanc-ti - fy me.
Where His glo-ry for - ev - er I'll share.

So I'll cher-ish the old rug-ged
cross, the

cross, ... Till my tro-phies at last I lay down; I will cling to the
old rugged cross,

old rug-ged cross, ... And ex-change it some day for a crown.
cross, the old rug-ged cross,

I Need Thee Every Hour.

Mrs. Annie S. Hawks.   Robert Lowry.

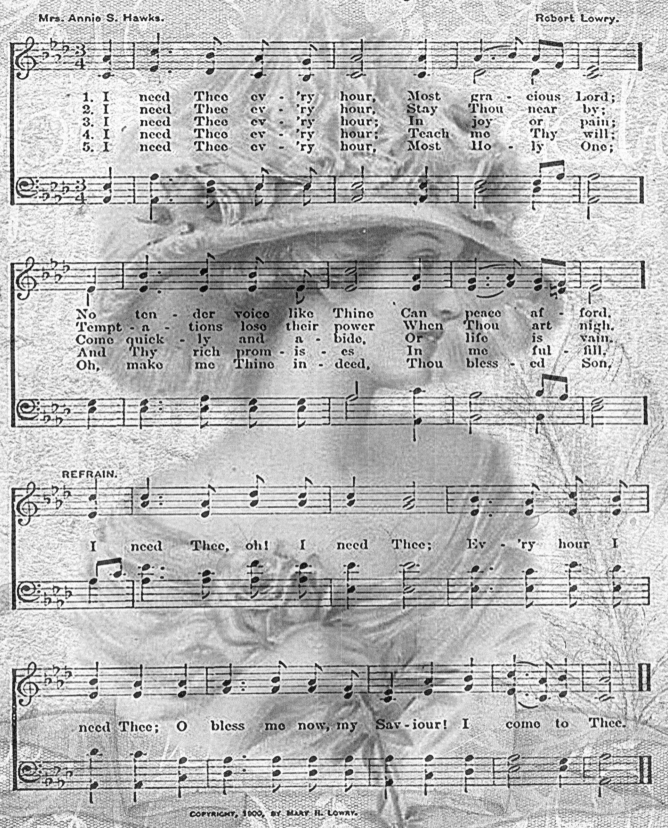

1. I need Thee ev-'ry hour, Most gra - cious Lord;
2. I need Thee ev-'ry hour, Stay Thou near by;
3. I need Thee ev-'ry hour; In joy or pain;
4. I need Thee ev-'ry hour; Teach me Thy will;
5. I need Thee ev-'ry hour, Most Ho - ly One;

No ten - der voice like Thine Can peace af - ford.
Tempt - a - tions lose their power When Thou art nigh.
Come quick - ly and a - bide, Or life is vain.
And Thy rich prom - is - es In me ful - fill.
Oh, make me Thine in - deed, Thou bless - ed Son,

REFRAIN.

I need Thee, oh! I need Thee; Ev - 'ry hour I

need Thee; O bless me now, my Sav - iour! I come to Thee.

All Hail the Power of Jesus' Name

WORDS: Edward Perronet, 1779; alt. John Rippon, 1787
MUSIC: Oliver Holden, 1792

CORONATION
CM with repeat

The First Noel

MODERATELY

Traditional

1. The first No - el, the an-gels did say, Was to cer-tain poor
2. They look - ed up and saw a star shin-ing in the
3. Then en - tered in the wise - men three, Full rev - er - ent-

shep-herds in fields as they lay; In fields where they lay
east, be - yond them far, And so the earth it
ly up - on their knee, And of - fered there, in

keep-ing their sheep, On a cold win-ter's night that was so deep.
gave great light, And so it con-tin-ued both day and night.
His pres-ence, Their gold and myrrh and frank - in - cense.

REFRAIN.

No - el, No - el, No - el, No - el, Born is the King of Is - ra - el.

This medieval Shepherd's tune first appeared in print in England and is, the reader will note, the story of the Nativity as told to the Shepherds by an angel

There is Power in the Blood.

L. E. J.   L. E. Jones.

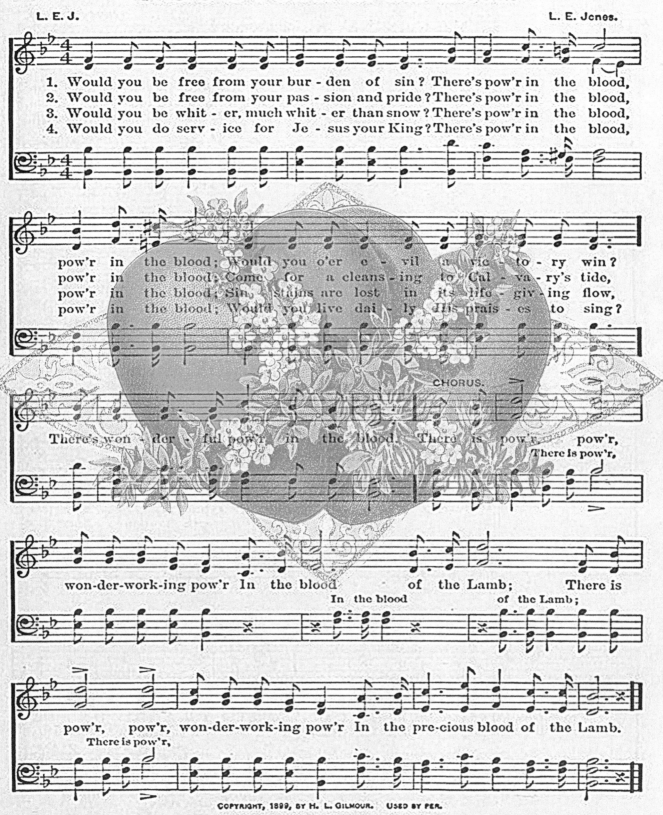

1. Would you be free from your bur - den of sin? There's pow'r in the blood,
2. Would you be free from your pas - sion and pride? There's pow'r in the blood,
3. Would you be whit - er, much whit - er than snow? There's pow'r in the blood,
4. Would you do serv - ice for Je - sus your King? There's pow'r in the blood,

pow'r in the blood; Would you o'er e - vil a vic - to - ry win?
pow'r in the blood; Come for a cleans - ing to Cal - va - ry's tide,
pow'r in the blood; Sin-stains are lost in its life - giv - ing flow,
pow'r in the blood; Would you live dai - ly His prais - es to sing?

CHORUS.

There's won - der - ful pow'r in the blood. There is pow'r pow'r,
There is pow'r,

won - der - work - ing pow'r In the blood of the Lamb; There is
In the blood of the Lamb;

pow'r, pow'r, won - der - work - ing pow'r In the pre - cious blood of the Lamb.
There is pow'r,

Stand Up, Stand Up for Jesus

GEORGE DUFFIELD, JR., 1818-1888   GEORGE J. WEBB, 1803-1887

1. Stand up, stand up for Je - sus, Ye sol - diers of the cross;
2. Stand up, stand up for Je - sus, The trum - pet call o - bey;
3. Stand up, stand up for Je - sus, Stand in his strength a - lone;
4. Stand up, stand up for Je - sus, The strife will not be long;

Lift high his roy - al ban - ner, It must not suf - fer loss;
Forth to the might - y con - flict, In this his glo - rious day;
The arm of flesh will fail you, Ye dare not trust your own;
This day the noise of bat - tle, The next, the vic - tor's song;

From vic - tory un - to vic - tory His ar - my shall he lead,
Ye that are men now serve him A - gainst un - num - bered foes;
Put on the gos - pel ar - mor, Each piece put on with prayer;
To him that o - ver - com - eth, A crown of life shall be;

Till ev - ery foe is van - quished, And Christ is Lord in - deed.
Let cour - age rise with dan - ger, And strength to strength op - pose.
Where du - ty calls or dan - ger, Be nev - er want - ing there.
He with the King of glo - ry Shall reign e - ter - nal - ly. A - men.

THE LORD'S PRAYER.

Andante.

E. O. EXCELL.

Our Father who art in heaven, Hal-low-ed be thy name, Thy
king-dom come, Thy will be done, in earth as it is in heaven,
Give us this day our dai - ly bread, And for-give us our debts, as
we for-give our debt-ors, And lead us not in - to temp-ta - tion;
but de - liv - er us from e - vil, For thine is the king-dom,
And the pow - er, and the glo-ry, for - ev - er, A - - men.

From "The Gospel in Song," by per.

When We All Get to Heaven

"In my Father's house are many mansions...I am going away to prepare a place for you." John 14:2

1. Sing the won-drous love of Je-sus, Sing His mer-cy and His grace;
2. While we walk the pil-grim path-way Clouds will o-ver-spread the sky;
3. Let us then be true and faith-ful, Trust-ing, serv-ing ev-'ry day;
4. On-ward to the prize be-fore us! Soon His beau-ty we'll be-hold;

In the man-sions bright and bless-ed He'll pre-pare for us a place.
But when trav-'ling days are o-ver, Not a shad-ow, not a sigh.
Just one glimpse of Him in glo-ry Will the toils of life re-pay.
Soon the pearl-y gates will o-pen; We shall tread the streets of gold.

1. for us a place.

Chorus

When we all get to heav-en, What a day of re-
When we all What a

joic-ing that will be! When we all see
day of re-joic-ing that will be! When we all

Je-sus. We'll sing and shout the vic-to-ry.
shout, and shout the vic-to-ry.

(segue)

WORDS: Eliza E. Hewitt
MUSIC: Emily D. Wilson

HEAVEN
8.7.8.7. with Chorus

'Tis So Sweet to Trust in Jesus

Louisa M. R. Stead, c. 1850-1917

William J. Kirkpatrick, 1838-1921

1. 'Tis so sweet to trust in Je - sus, And to take him at his word;
2. O how sweet to trust in Je - sus, Just to trust his cleans-ing blood;
3. Yes, 'tis sweet to trust in Je - sus, Just from sin and self to cease;
4. I'm so glad I learned to trust thee, Pre-cious Je - sus, Sav-ior, friend;

Just to rest up - on his prom-ise, And to know, "Thus saith the Lord."
And in sim - ple faith to plunge me Neath the heal - ing, cleans-ing flood!
Just from Je - sus sim - ply tak - ing Life and rest, and joy and peace.
And I know that thou art with me, Wilt be with me to the end.

Refrain

Je - sus, Je - sus, how I trust him! How I've proved him o'er and o'er!

Je - sus, Je - sus, pre-cious Je - sus! O for grace to trust him more! A-men.

THOMAS KEN   DOXOLOGY   LOUIS BOURGEOIS

Praise God, from whom all blessings flow; Praise Him, all crea-tures here be - low;

Praise Him a - bove, ye heaven-ly host; Praise Fa-ther, Son, and Ho - ly Ghost.

Jesus Loves the Little Children.

Anon.   Geo. F. Root.

Je - sus loves the lit - tle chil - dren, All the chil-dren of the

world; Red and yel - low, black and white, They are

pre-cious in His sight; Je - sus loves the lit - tle chil-dren of the world.

No. 37. Tell Me the Old, Old Story.

"Tell them how great things the Lord hath done."—MARK 5: 19.

Miss KATE HANKEY.

W. H. DOANE, by per.

1. Tell me the Old, Old Sto - ry, Of un-seen things a - bove, Of
2. Tell me the Sto - ry slow - ly, That I may take it in— That

Je - sus and His glo - ry, Of Je - sus and His love. Tell me the Sto-ry
wonder-ful re - demp-tion, God's rem-e-dy for sin. Tell me the Sto-ry

sim - ply, As to a lit - tle child, For I am weak and wea - ry, And
oft - en, For I for-get so soon, The "early dew" of morn-ing Has

CHORUS.

help - less and de - filed. Tell me the Old, Old Sto - ry, Tell me the Old, Old
passed a - way at noon.

Sto - ry, Tell me the Old, Old Sto - ry Of Je - sus and His love.

JESUS PAID IT ALL.

Mrs. E. M. Hall.   John T. Grape.

1. I hear the Saviour say, "Thy strength indeed is small; Child of weakness,
2. Lord, now indeed I find Thy pow'r, and Thine alone, Can change the
3. For nothing good have I Where-by Thy grace to claim—I'll wash my

CHORUS.

watch and pray, Find in me thine all in all."
lep - er's spots, And melt the heart of stone. Je - sus paid it all,
gar-ments white In the blood of Cal-v'ry's Lamb.

All to Him I owe; Sin had left a crimson stain, He washed it white as snow.

Away in A Manger

SLOWLY, GENTLY

A - way in a man-ger, no crib for His bed, The lit-tle Lord
The cat-tle are low-ing, the poor Ba - by wakes, But lit-tle Lord

Je - sus laid down His sweet head. The stars in the sky look-ing
Je - sus, no cry - ing He makes. I love Thee, Lord Je sus; look

down where He lay, The lit - tle Lord Je - sus a - sleep in the hay.
down from the sky, And stay by my crib, watch-ing my lul - la - by.

50 Christ Arose.

Robert Lowry.

Robert Lowry.

1. Low in the grave He lay— Je-sus my Sav-ior! Wait-ing the com-ing day—
2. Vain-ly they watch His bed—Je-sus my Sav-ior! Vain-ly they seal the dead—
3. Death can-not keep his prey—Je-sus my Sav-ior! He tore the bars a'-way—

REFRAIN. *Faster.*

Je-sus my Lord! Up from the grave He a-rose, (He a-rose,) With a

might-y tri-umph o'er His foes; (He a-rose!) He a-rose a Vic-tor from the

dark do-main, And He lives for-ev-er with His saints to reign. He a-

rose! He a-rose! Hal-le-lu-jah! Christ a-rose! A-MEN

He a-rose! He a-rose!

206 Joy In My Heart.

Arr. by B. B. McKinney.

1. I have the joy! joy! joy! joy! down in my heart, Down in my heart, Down in my heart,
2. I have the peace that passeth understanding, down in my heart, Down in my heart, Down in my heart,
3. I have the love of Je - sus down in my heart, Down in my heart, Down in my heart,

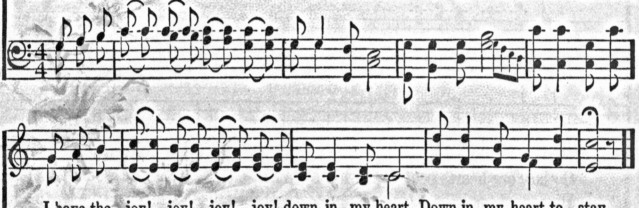

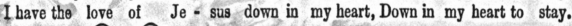

I have the joy! joy! joy! joy! down in my heart, Down in my heart to stay.
I have the peace that passeth understanding, down in my heart, Down in my heart to stay.
I have the love of Je - sus down in my heart, Down in my heart to stay.

We Gather Together

Netherlands Folk Hymn

Nederlandtsch Gedenckclanck, 1626
Arr. by EDWARD KREMSER, 1838-1914

1. We gath-er to-geth-er to ask the Lord's bless-ing;
2. Be-side us to guide us, our God with us join-ing,
3. We all do ex-tol thee, thou lead-er tri-um-phant,

He chas-tens and has-tens his will to make known;
Or-dain-ing, main-tain-ing his king-dom di-vine;
And pray that thou still our de-fend-er wilt be.

The wick-ed op-press-ing now cease from dis-tress-ing,
So from the be-gin-ning the fight we were win-ning;
Let thy con-gre-ga-tion es-cape trib-u-la-tion;

Sing prais-es to his name: He for-gets not his own.
Thou, Lord, wast at our side, All glo-ry be thine!
Thy name be ev-er praised! O Lord, make us free! A-men.

I Shall Not Be Moved.

Arr. by B. B. McK.   Arr. by B. B. McKinney.

1. Je - sus saves for-ev - er,   I shall not be moved; He will leave me nev - er,
2. On His grace re - ly-ing,   I shall not be moved; For His love un - dy-ing,
3. With the Church I'm going, I shall not be moved; Christ to lost ones showing,
4. From the Word e-ter - nal   I shall not be moved; From its truth su-per-nal

I shall not be moved; Just like a tree that's planted by the wa - ter,
I shall not be moved; Just like a tree that's planted by the wa - ter,
I shall not be moved; Just like a tree that's planted by the wa - ter,
I shall not be moved; Just like a tree that's planted by the wa - ter,

CHORUS.

I shall not be moved.   I shall not be, I shall not be moved;

I shall   not be,   I shall not be moved; Just like a

tree that's planted by the wa - ter,   I shall not be moved.

When the Saints Go Marching In.

Words adapted and
Written by B. B. McK

Arr. by B. B. McKinney.

1. I had a lov-ing broth-er, Death re-leased him from sin,
2. I had a pre-cious sis-ter, She has gone on be-fore,
3. I have a Christ-like fa-ther, Far be-yond the blue skies,
4. I have a dear, sweet moth-er, Sing-ing 'round the white throne,
5. I have a liv-ing Sav-ior, He re-deemed me from sin;

And I prom-ised I would meet him, When the saints go march-ing in.
And I prom-ised I would meet her On that hap-py, gold-en shore.
And some day I'll sure-ly meet him, Where there'll be no sad good-byes.
And I prom-ised I would meet her; "There we'll know as we are known."
Oh, how sweet 'twill be to meet Him, When the saints go march-ing in.

CHORUS.

When the saints . . . . . go march-ing in, ...
Oh, when the saints go march-ing in,

When the saints go march-ing in; . . . . . Lord, I want to
go march-ing in;

be in that num-ber, ... When the saints go marching in.
in that num-ber,

SS—4

94 Since Jesus Came Into My Heart.

R. H. McDaniel.

Chas. H. Gabriel.

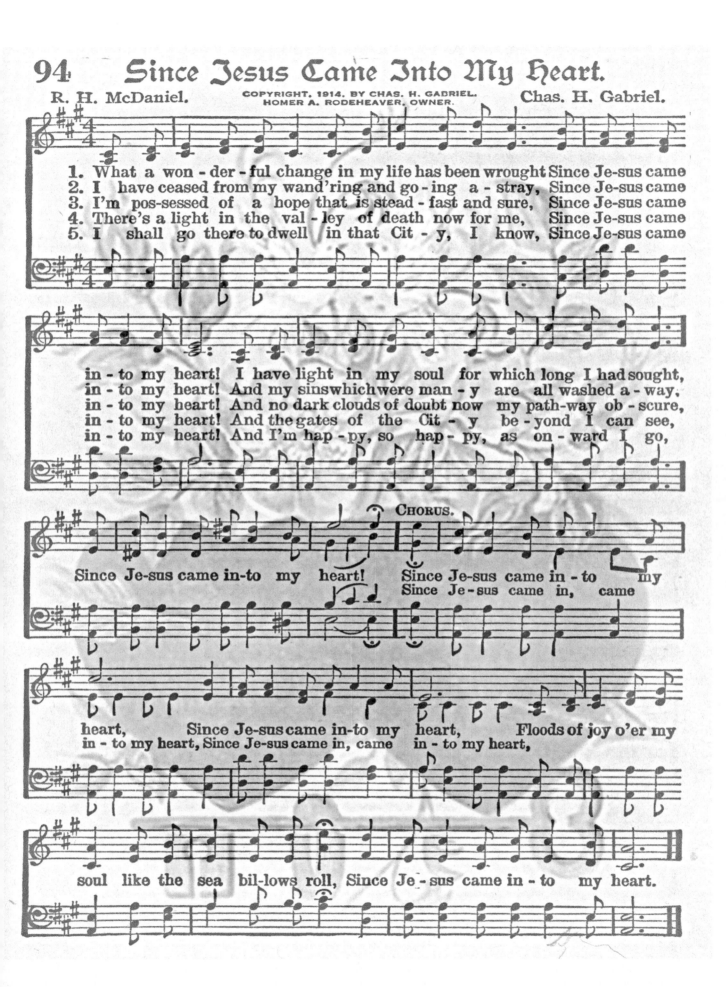

1. What a won-der-ful change in my life has been wrought Since Je-sus came
2. I have ceased from my wand'ring and go-ing a-stray, Since Je-sus came
3. I'm pos-sessed of a hope that is stead-fast and sure, Since Je-sus came
4. There's a light in the val-ley of death now for me, Since Je-sus came
5. I shall go there to dwell in that Cit-y, I know, Since Je-sus came

in-to my heart! I have light in my soul for which long I had sought,
in-to my heart! And my sins which were man-y are all washed a-way,
in-to my heart! And no dark clouds of doubt now my path-way ob-scure,
in-to my heart! And the gates of the Cit-y be-yond I can see,
in-to my heart! And I'm hap-py, so hap-py, as on-ward I go,

CHORUS.

Since Je-sus came in-to my heart! Since Je-sus came in-to my
Since Je-sus came in, came

heart, Since Je-sus came in-to my heart, Floods of joy o'er my
in-to my heart, Since Je-sus came in, came in-to my heart,

soul like the sea bil-lows roll, Since Je-sus came in-to my heart.

Rock of Ages, Cleft for Me

Augustus M. Toplady, 1740-1778

Thomas Hastings, 1784-1872

1. Rock of A - ges, cleft for me, Let me
2. Could my tears for - ev - er flow, Could my
3. While I draw this fleet - ing breath, When my

hide my - self in thee; Let the wa - ter and the blood,
zeal no lan - guor know, These for sin could not a - tone;
eyes shall close in death, When I rise to worlds un - known,

From thy wound - ed side which flowed, Be of sin the dou - ble
Thou must save, and thou a - lone. In my hand no price I
And be - hold thee on thy throne, Rock of A - ges, cleft for

cure, Save from wrath and make me pure.
bring; Sim - ply to thy cross I cling.
me, Let me hide my - self in thee. A - men.

The Solid Rock

They drank from the spiritual rock ... Christ — 1 Corinthians 10:4 NIV

1. My hope is built on noth-ing less Than Je-sus' blood and righ-teous-ness;
2. When dark-ness seems to hide His face, I rest on His un-chang-ing grace;
3. His oath, His cov-e-nant, His blood Sup-port me in the whelm-ing flood;
4. When He shall come with trum-pet sound, Oh, may I then in Him be found;

I dare not trust the sweet-est frame, But whol-ly lean on Je-sus' name.
In ev-'ry high and storm-y gale, My an-chor holds with-in the veil.
When all a-round my soul gives way, He then is all my hope and stay.
Dressed in His right-teous-ness a-lone, Fault-less to stand be-fore the throne.

On Christ, the sol-id Rock, I stand; All oth-er ground is

sink-ing sand, All oth-er ground is sink-ing sand.

WORDS: Edward Mote, 1797-1874
MUSIC: William B. Bradbury, 1816-1868

SOLID ROCK
8.8.8.8.(L.M.) with Refrain

THIS LITTLE LIGHT OF MINE

The B-I-B-L-E

The B - I - B - L - E, Yes
The B - I - B - L - E, I'll
By F - A - I - T - H, I'm

that's the book for me. I
take it a - long with me, I'll
S - A - V - E - D, I'll

stand a - lone on the Word of God, The
read and pray, and then o - bey, The
stand a - lone on the World of God, The

B - I - B - L - E.
B - I - B - L - E.
B - I - B - L - E.

Made in the USA
Las Vegas, NV
07 January 2022